CHRISTOPHER WILMARTH

LAURA ROSENSTOCK

THE MUSEUM OF MODERN ART NEW YORK

CHRISTOPHER WILMARTH

LAURA ROSENSTOCK

THE MUSEUM OF MODERN ART NEW YORK

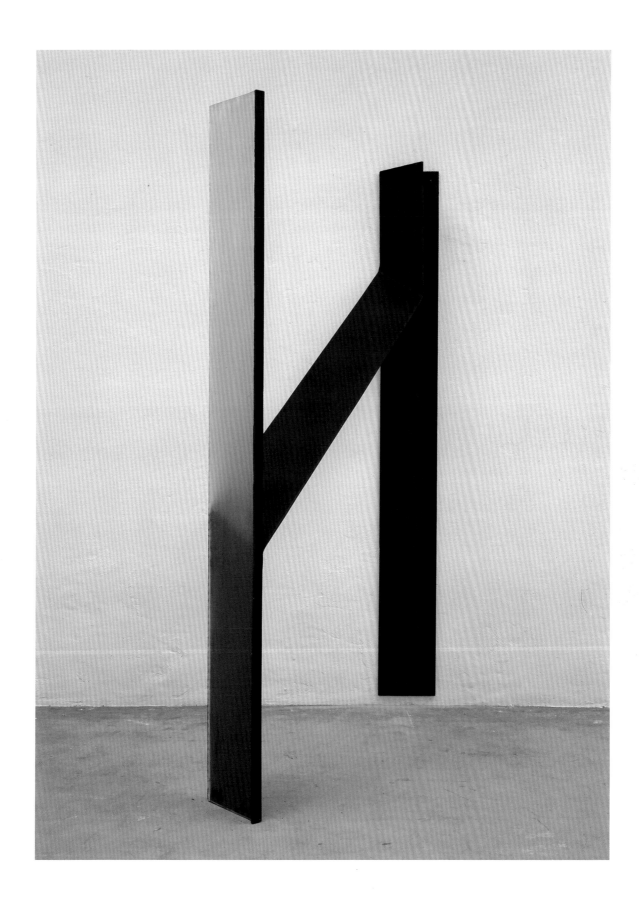

Published on the occasion of
the exhibition "Christopher Wilmarth"
The Museum of Modern Art, New York
May 25–August 22, 1989

The exhibition and this publication have been made possible by
a generous grant from Edward R. Broida.

Library of Congress Catalogue Card Number 89-870706
ISBN 0-87070-644-6

Edited by Maura Walsh
Designed by Gregory Gillbergh
Production by Pamela S. Smith
Composition by Maxwell Typographers, Inc., New York
Printed by Village Craftsmen/Princeton Polychrome Press,
New Jersey
Bound by Mueller Trade Bindery, Middletown,
Connecticut

Cover: *Is, Was (Chancing)*. 1975–76

Frontispiece: *Gnomon's Parade (Front)*. 1980

The Museum of Modern Art
11 West 53 Street
New York, New York 10019

Photograph Credits

The following list is keyed to plate numbers and, where relevant,
figure numbers.

Kate Keller, Staff Photographer, The Museum of Modern Art:
14, 15, 17, 21, 22, 25, 30, 31, 34, 35, 36; Robert E. Mates and
Paul Katz, New York: 10, 11, 12; James Mathews: fig. 4;
courtesy Pierre Matisse Gallery, New York: fig. 3; Mali Olatunji,
Staff Photographer, The Museum of Modern Art: 4, 33; © 1989
Douglas M. Parker, Los Angeles: 3; Eric Pollitzer, New York:
19, 20, 27, figs. 2, 6; Jerry L. Thompson, Amenia, New York:
cover, frontispiece, 1, 2, 5 (courtesy Hirschl & Adler Modern,
New York), 6, 7, 9, 13, 16, 18, 23, 24, 26, 28, 29, 32, 37, 38,
figs. 1, 5; © Malcolm Varon, New York: fig. 8; courtesy Walker
Art Center, Minneapolis: 8.

Printed in the United States of America
Second Printing, 1989

CONTENTS

FOREWORD

Christopher Wilmarth's finest sculptures involve a magic worked in full view. A few simply inflected elements of steel and glass conjure a range of light, scale, space, and weight, which in turn alludes to experiences of place, time, and—more difficult still to define—presence. No matter how often in modern art's history we have seen it, we may still feel wonder at such alchemy, by which an artist can make, from the seemingly intractable means of geometric shapes and industrial materials, a personal poetry of subtle and meditative effect. Formal reduction here is a way not to nail down absolutes but to compress complex sensations that would be betrayed by more elaborate description.

Much of the best-known sculpture of the seventies worked with dispersal as its strategy, and nature as its concern. But Wilmarth's hallmark was condensation, and his subject was the city. Urban light, slanting through building slots into empty spaces, or diffracting through scuffed and pebbled windows, can at times order the accreted collage of New York into new and unexpected unities, and offer with them moments of singular reverie. Wilmarth's etched-glass and steel pieces hold in poise the contradictions of those epiphanies, of pleasure and melancholy, intimacy and scale, fragility and power, present-tense clarity and transported rumination.

In treating such experiences Wilmarth remade something of what he admired of Symbolist poetry, but in contemporary terms that married two very different sensibilities. Part of the work's spareness reaffirms an attitude we associate with New York Minimalism: the idea that, when we strip away all frills, we get sharply defined, elemental forms that square with the hard categories of the logical mind. But another part belongs to a fascination with light and space that characterized Minimalism on the West Coast: there, stripping away meant losing the definition of forms in a dissolving field, where the margins of sensory perception led away from the rational to the transcendent.

With that tectonic purity, though, Wilmarth's pieces also have a lithe energy, a step or pace, that belies any ponderous solemnity. Some of the titles, too—*Tina Turner*, or homages to Hank Williams—reaffirm that this art was not cloistered but engaged with the complexities of life. It was urbane as well as urban, at home with an aesthetic where French poetry and Memphis music could coexist as naturally as they do in so many contemporary experiences. This special serenity is what disappears, however, in the troubling imagery of his last works. As the forms of the body take over from those of the city, and the variety of light begins to be replaced by nocturnes, the rhetorical tone of Wilmarth's sculptures and drawings changes dramatically, and ultimately tragically.

Wilmarth's works of the early eighties seem to take part in a broader shift in the art world around him, toward painterly expressionism. But they are utterly lacking in the ironic, eclectic tone that characterized much of that expressionism in contemporary painting. Instead, these autobiographically charged pieces willfully negate a personal set of forms: opacity smothers translucency, surface occludes depth, and symbolic persona (the isolated, floating head) displaces intuited presence (the standing man) in his family of surrogate signs. What began in blond wood and clear glass, and matured in the subtle lucidity of steel and etched planes, ended here in dark bronze and covering lead, with the artist still mapping a deeply personal itinerary in a land of light and shadow.

Kirk Varnedoe, Director
Department of Painting and Sculpture
The Museum of Modern Art

ACKNOWLEDGMENTS

A completed exhibition should leave no trace of the difficulties involved in its organization and installation. But difficulties there are, on every level, and these few lines offer us the occasion to acknowledge the individuals who overcame these impediments—of expense, of time, of logistics—in order to present the art of Christopher Wilmarth. Our primary debt of gratitude is owed to Edward R. Broida. His immediate understanding of the importance of our project for a Wilmarth show, and his extraordinarily generous willingness to assume the costs of a display and catalogue that would do justice to the artist's achievement, provided the indispensable base of support for the show. The level of his commitment challenged and inspired everyone involved. Secondly, we wish to thank those who graciously consented to lend works from their collection to the exhibition. As Wilmarth's works are often delicate and potentially vulnerable, we are especially appreciative of the loans accorded by: Robert and Marlene Baumgarten; The Edward R. Broida Trust, Los Angeles; Asher B. Edelman, New York; George G. Hadley and Richard L. Solomon; Robert Lehrman, Washington, D.C.; Mr. and Mrs. David Pincus; Stephen D. Weinroth, New York; the Estate of Christopher Wilmarth, New York; Susan Wilmarth, New York; Wadsworth Atheneum, Hartford; Walker Art Center, Minneapolis; Philadelphia Museum of Art; and Hirschl & Adler Modern, New York; as well as a number of lenders who wish to remain anonymous. Finally, great credit and appreciation are due Laura Rosenstock, Assistant Curator in the Department of Painting and Sculpture, for organizing the exhibition and this publication, and for her insightful essay. Her work has been done with wonderful efficiency, as well as with intense concern for the quality of the art and the significance of the issues involved. The achievement is all the more remarkable for having been realized under exceptionally strong constraints of time, and we offer her warmest thanks and congratulations.

K. V.

My very warm thanks are due first to Susan Wilmarth. Her special insights into Christopher Wilmarth's work have been invaluable, and I am deeply grateful for her kind cooperation and patient collaboration. My appreciation is also extended to Betty Cuningham of Hirschl & Adler Modern, who has willingly assisted in locating works and enthusiastically provided needed information. Ingrid Schaffner has given generously of her time and archival expertise, Jerry L. Thompson provided much of the necessary photography, and Tom Delano has shared his special knowledge of the handling and installation of the sculptures; I thank them. Tracie Felker, Susan Halper, Donald McKinney, William McNaught, Marc Selwyn, and Linda Thacher also have my sincere gratitude.

Within the Department of Painting and Sculpture, I would like especially to acknowledge the contribution of Mary Beth Smalley, Curatorial Assistant. She has been an invaluable colleague, collaborating with enthusiasm and critical intelligence in all aspects of the exhibition and catalogue. She coordinated the exhibition history and bibliographic material for this publication, and her help is deeply appreciated. I am grateful as well to Julia McNeil, who gathered much needed documentation and assisted in countless other ways, always with professionalism, efficiency, and good humor. My thanks go also to Linda Shearer and Carolyn Lanchner, Curators, for their advice and assistance, to Kynaston McShine, Senior Curator, for his continued encouragement, and to Kirk Varnedoe, Director of the Department, for his unqualified support of this undertaking.

Many other colleagues at the Museum have been generous in lending their talent and expertise. I would particularly like to thank Richard E. Oldenburg, Director of the Museum, and James Snyder, Deputy Director for Planning and Program Support, for their interest and support. John Elderfield, Director of the Department of Drawings, was also especially encouraging. Richard L. Palmer and Betsy Jablow, respectively Coordinator and Associate Coordinator of Exhibitions, ably supervised scheduling and budgetary matters, and Jerome Neuner, Production Manager, lent his expert attention to the installation of the art. Sarah Tappen, Assistant Registrar, coordinated complicated shipping arrangements. Antoinette King, Director of Conservation, and conservators Patricia Houlihan and Lynda Zycherman were of special assistance. I extend appreciation as well to Sue B. Dorn, Jeanne Collins, Edna Goldstaub, Eloise Ricciardelli, Karen Meyerhoff, Fred Coxen, and Rosette Bakish.

Finally, I wish to acknowledge a special debt to the members of the Department of Publications for the preparation of this catalogue. Maura Walsh edited the manuscript with perception, and Gregory Gillbergh contributed the book's handsome design. Tim McDonough and Pamela S. Smith have overseen this volume's production with skilled professionalism. Harriet Bee, Nancy Kranz, and Michael Hentges likewise contributed in important ways, as did Richard Tooke, Mikki Carpenter, Kate Keller, and Mali Olatunji. The expertise and assistance of all are deeply appreciated.

L.R.

CHRISTOPHER WILMARTH
AN INTRODUCTION

Light gains character as it touches the world; from what is lighted and who is there to see. I associate the significant moments of my life with the character of light at the time. The universal implications of my original experience have located in and become signified by kinds of light. My sculptures are places to generate this experience compressed into light and shadow and return them to the world as a physical poem.[1]

—Christopher Wilmarth

Christopher Wilmarth's art drew above all else on his concern with the mystical and physical possibilities of light—on the ways in which light can evoke reverie and inner longings and generate varied sensations of space and containment. His poems, his prose descriptions of walking through New York City's streets toward its rivers and onto its bridges, indeed his entire artistic sensibility derived from his desire to express his experience of light. It is somewhat paradoxical that Wilmarth should have sought to suggest this immaterial world of light, and shadow, by combining massive industrial materials: plate glass, sheet steel, steel cable. Nonetheless, his sculpture is remarkable in its ability to convey his feelings for subtle modulations of light and shadow, and to intimate poetic, even romantic content through an austerely constructivist, geometric idiom.

Wilmarth transformed his raw materials by treating glass and steel in a manner associated more with a pictorial tradition. In the seventies, especially, he composed with planes of delicate color and light, placing cut-and-bent plates of dark, shadowy steel behind translucent sheets of etched glass imbued with a painterly surface and a luminous, greenish cast. He thought of his structures as "places," and he invested them with a human presence. That presence is implied either through the scale, shape, and vulnerability of the work, or, with a more visible sense of self-reflexiveness, through the use of a symbolic ovoid form. Distinguished by their fusion of fragility and strength, these pieces transcend their visual beauty and open up a realm of meditation and imagination.

Wilmarth was born in 1943 in Sonoma, California, and grew up in the Bay Area. In 1960 he moved to New York, a city that would serve as a great stimulus for his art. He sought to evoke in sculpture the qualities of light and shadow characteristic of New York's sky and water. At The Cooper Union for the Advancement of Science and Art, Wilmarth was drawn to the sculpture of Constantin Brancusi. Brancusi's love of rough-hewn wood, his tendency to conjoin wood with polished metal or stone, and his infusion of metaphysical significance into simple,

Figure 1: Her Sides of Me. *1964. Wood and cement, 6′8″ × 25¹/₂″ × 15″ (203.2 × 64.8 × 38.1 cm). Estate of Christopher Wilmarth, New York*

reductive forms had a strong impact on Wilmarth. Brancusi's legacy, so clearly evident in the carved-wood shapes of Wilmarth's student sculpture (figure 1), extended as well into his later sculptural investigations.

Wilmarth was also attracted to the art of Henri Matisse, in whose work, as in that of Brancusi, he sensed a deeply humanist expression. Wilmarth's early drawings (figure 2) testify to his admiration for the sensual line and deep shading that shapes the light of the white paper in Matisse's charcoal figure studies of the thirties and forties. Wilmarth's sculptures of the seventies, luminous presences suggestive of landscape and rich in poetic intensity, attest to the continued influence of Matisse, and especially recall that artist's partially abstract 1914 window paintings (figure 3).[2]

Also influential for Wilmarth was Tony Smith, for whom he worked as a studio assistant for two years, helping to build, install, and paint Smith's wood prototypes. While Smith's reductive, geometric vocabulary was a model for Wilmarth, Wilmarth felt the minimalistic aesthetic was not relevant to his own artistic concerns. Other sources and affinities range from the paintings of Edward Hopper, which, like Wilmarth's sculptures, frequently explore the emotive effects of light in architectonic settings, to the drawings and paintings of Alberto Giacometti, whose elongated figures isolated on grisaille backgrounds are alluded to in Wilmarth's last drawings (1987; figure 8, plates 33–36). Finally, Wilmarth's pictorial use of light and shadow, as well as the spiritual quality of his art, have caused certain of his works to be compared to Rothko's late black-and-gray paintings.

Yet however much he was inspired by this eclectic combination of influences, Wilmarth developed a body of work that was defined by a unique personal vision and was not bound by any movement or category. Engaging in an intuitive, expressive process, and referring to aspects of his environment and life, Wilmarth created pieces that developed out of and built directly upon one another. His oeuvre was shaped by an overridingly consistent sensibility discernible throughout his art in several areas. He employed a painterly technique that emphasized the tactility and richness of his materials, which like an alchemist he persistently sought to transform. He continually examined the concept of duality: contrasts between light and shadow, transparency and opacity, heaviness and weightlessness, materiality and ethereality, form and spirit are repeatedly presented; the synthesis of geometric with organic forms, the range between abstraction and representation are constantly explored. He endowed his sculptures with a sense of "place" and "person," which was as critical to his intention as was his lifelong concern with the evocative power of light.

The vehicle that Wilmarth felt could best capture the experience of light—his true medium—was glass. His first works employing glass date from 1967 and are composed of unpainted spools and partial cylinders of birch plywood sliced by plate glass. While the emphasis of these pieces remained on the wood veneer—a natural outgrowth of his everyday work at that time as a cabinetmaker, and of course, the continued influence of Brancusi[3]—they did, nevertheless, establish two tenets that would continue to inform Wilmarth's art: the use of disparate materials and shapes—round wood volumes and planar, transparent glass—and the inversion or transformation of these materials. The plywood, while seemingly weighty and solid, is actually light and hollow; the fragile-looking glass is thick and heavy.

Throughout 1969 and 1970 Wilmarth experimented with glass in ways previ-

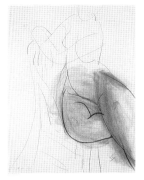

Figure 2: Yolande. 1965. Charcoal on paper, 24³/₈ × 18⁷/₈" (61.9 × 47.9 cm). Estate of Christopher Wilmarth, New York

Figure 3: Henri Matisse. View of Notre Dame. 1914. Oil on canvas, 58 × 37¹/₈" (147.3 × 94.3 cm). The Museum of Modern Art, New York. Acquired through the Lillie P. Bliss Bequest, and the Henry Ittleson, A. Conger Goodyear, and Mr. and Mrs. Robert Sinclair Funds, and the Anna Erickson Levene Bequest given in memory of her husband, Dr. Phoebus Aaron Theodor Levene

ously unexplored in sculpture. Absorbed by glass's many possibilities, among them its ability to retain its form yet transmit light, he visited manufacturers, observed the entire production process, examined the various hues and thicknesses available. He discovered that the medium could be cut, bent, curved, shaped, stacked, chipped, suspended, layered—and etched.

By etching the surface of glass with hydrofluoric acid, Wilmarth found, he could intensify the greenish tint immanent in the glass while replacing its transparency and reflectivity with a frosted translucency. As before, he continued to alter the properties of his materials: what once transmitted light now retained it, and the etched-glass pieces glowed with a radiant green luminosity. In these works, the unevenly brushed-on acid yields a seductively soft, irregular, painterly surface, which is delicately suffused with color, ranging from an elusive ice green to a glowing greenish blue, that changes with the light and the movement of the viewer. The green tone gains depth with the increasing thickness of the glass; edges are greener than frontal planes. When plates are overlapped, further nuances of translucency, deepening hues, and secondary tones result.

The etching process was fundamental to Wilmarth's work. Because this method enabled him to control the degree of transparency in the glass, each piece could take on a different and individual character. Some works, almost opaque, are opalescent in color like frost on a window. Some, like *Susan Walked In* (1972; plate 9), are etched in all directions in a "Matissean" scumble that allows glints of light to shine through. Others, like *Blue Time Line* (1974; plate 16), are etched more evenly in a single direction, and present a soft, matte, all-over "field" that exudes a rich sea-green coloration.

By 1970 Wilmarth had introduced another pictorial element into his sculpture: Roebling steel suspension cable (invented by John A. Roebling, designer of the Brooklyn Bridge). This black cable serves both structural and compositional functions, supporting the glass panes and binding them to one another, to the wall, and later to steel even as it acts as a type of scribed line. (The staples Wilmarth employed in his drawings [plates 14 and 15] serve a similar role, joining the layers of paper together and giving linear definition.)[4] The dual function of the cable is prefigured in the whimsical, ostensibly casual *Thinner* (1969–70; plate 7), in which multiple glass disks are strung on and held up by slender steel rods, which also give the work a linear configuration. The threaded ridges of the rods echo the spiraling motion of the disks in a playful fashion. The piece is an enticing study in balance, gravity, and weight.

Acting as a taut, strong support, the Roebling cable nonetheless becomes a form of delicate drawing. It focuses attention on other contradictions as well: the seeming weightlessness of the glass is contrasted with its actual heaviness and tensile strength when the tightly drawn cable reveals the pull of gravity. While it is pictorial in an almost two-dimensional sense, the steel cable serves also to project the viewer three-dimensionally behind the glass as he attempts to follow its course through the various panes.

As with the various techniques of etching, the black line of the cable adds articulation to the glass in ways that individualize each piece. In *Lace* (1972; plate 6) the cable twists illogically in and out of eight different holes, sometimes singly, sometimes in multiple loops. In *Untied Drawing* (1971; plate 5) it methodically weaves two plates together in long vertical patterns. In *Tarp* (1971; plate 4) the cable dramatically outlines two black rectangles against the wall, which serve as foils to the suspended arcs of glass seen on edge and almost invisible. This fine sense of equilibrium is beautifully expressed in *Little Bent Memphis* (1971; plate 3), where the curved horizontal sheet of glass appears to balance weightlessly from one asymmetrically placed string of cable that reaches high above it. That poised suspension, in conjunction with the atmospheric, cloudlike quality of the sculpture's etching, makes the work appear truly ethereal. In *Blue Time Line* the glass openly accommodates the supporting function of the cable. The cutout portion of the glass is a structural necessity, as it allows the steel to wrap underneath and suspend the bowed pane. The horizontal continuation of the cable, however, has no structural function; its role is purely visual, optically balancing the off-center vertical line and delineating a rectangle that counters the sensuous bend of the glass, calling to mind the rigging of a sail. The cable in *Tina Turner* (1970–71; plate 1) similarly serves to echo and enrich the shape of the sculpture, emphasizing its many contrasts of flat/round, in front/behind, translucent/transparent.

In 1971, seeking a broader palette of colors in his sculpture, Wilmarth first incorporated steel, in a collaborative piece executed with his friend Mark di Suvero. By the next year Wilmarth had added sheet steel to his vocabulary, layering plates of it behind glass panes.[5] This bringing together gave rise to some of Wilmarth's signature structures, works in which the materials engage in a particularly dynamic dialogue. In these pieces, the fragility of the glass and its seductive, luminous surface contrast with the brute power of the blackened steel. At the same time, this contrast appears to transform the nature of the materials themselves. While the glass assumes the strength and intensified color of the steel behind it, the heavy metal, its tones softened, blued, and partially obscured by the glass, becomes quiet, mysterious, and weightless, more shadow than substance.

The force of these works derives from the artist's poetic use of light and shadow. When a section of steel is cut or folded it traps and diffuses the light through the frosted glass, creating shifting spaces and multiple shadows of varying depths. The amount of variation Wilmarth achieved within this format is remarkable. The direction and location of the bending allow a variety of configurations of softly outlined forms, shadowed intersections, and gradations of light. When the glass and steel are close together gray-black metal predominates; when they are apart green etched glass is preeminent. Sometimes the wall can be glimpsed, as in *New Ninth* (1978; plate 24), where the central portion of the sculpture suggests a window with open shutters.

The eloquence and lyricism of Wilmarth's glass-and-steel pieces are nowhere more fully expressed than in the series *Nine Clearings for a Standing Man* (1973; plates 12 and 13), a set of works based on permutations of a vertical, rectangular shape. Each piece is composed of glass and steel plates of identical size, the variables being the angle at which the steel bends from the glass to admit light and the position and length of the cable. Dark green, glowing works, seen as if through a misty haze, they reverberate with an almost mystical aura that blurs edges into soft, white, shimmering tonalities. They suggest sky and light and recall Matisse's voluptuous shading and evocation of landscape.

Wilmarth thought of his sculptures as states of mind, "places" conveyed by light "that evoke a spiritual disembodied state close to that of reverie."[6] Each of the *Nine Clearings* structures has a distinct expressive character and engenders a particular meditative mood, as shadows yield to "clearings" of light. Within these "places" there is the suggestion of the human presence, "a standing man." In connection with his *Nine Clearings* series, Wilmarth wrote:

> *For years I have been concerned with the complex problem of implying the human presence in a non-objective art. The concept of the self-generated form approaches a*

13

Figure 4: Normal Corner (Yard). *1972. Steel and etched glass, 30³/₈ × 60¹/₈ × 30³/₈"* (*77.2 × 152.5 × 77.2 cm*). The Museum of Modern Art, New York. Given anonymously

solution in that the sculpture attains a living presence. The layering of material has organic implications but it was the feeling of people in places and the special energy certain places have long after the people have gone that provided insight into my concern with the figure. The configuration, scale and proportion of place can evoke human presence. These are the places I speak of when I say my sculptures are places to generate experience. The feeling is intimate. You are acknowledged.[7]

The *Nine Clearings* pieces allude to a human presence not only in their proportion and shape but also in the vulnerability and delicate balance of the glass and in the ephemeral, time-bound movements of shadow and light. These sculptures have extraordinary emotional resonance and poignancy, qualities that figure strongly through Wilmarth's last works.

Wilmarth's structures, while appearing pictorial and allusive, are nevertheless assertively three-dimensional constructions and activate real spaces behind, between, and around the glass and steel components. Even his early glass-and-cable reliefs, such as *Untied Drawing* and *Lace*, insist on their physicality, as the thick, multiple panes frequently overlap and the cable almost disappears behind the glass. Although the space between the glass and the wall in the *Nine Clearings* works is actually quite shallow (averaging only four inches), the viewer nonetheless experiences it as a tangible volume. And the larger floor pieces, in which the steel seems almost to shelter the glass, have a markedly architectonic character that enhances their three-dimensionality. In *Gift of the Bridge* (1975 –76; plate 19), for example, Wilmarth imaginatively employed the psychological and associative effects of space to evoke the structure of an altar or shelter that invites entry. The configuration of the piece and the quality of its light and shadow change dramatically when viewed from different angles. Here, as throughout his sculpture, Wilmarth endowed his artistic expression with both clarity and mystery, turning a structure that presupposes a constructivist propensity for contained space into an occasion for deep reverie.

Wilmarth's strong spatial sense clearly comes into play in his treatment of the steel rectangle. While all the intricacies of form evolve from cutting and bending the sheet, the implication of the original plate is usually conserved. Wilmarth wrote of retaining "the memory of the first form . . . in the completed piece, giving the sculpture a history."[8] In *Susan Walked In* or *Is, Was (Chancing)* (1975 – 76; plate 18) the viewer can mentally reconstruct the folds and cuts by which Wilmarth arrived at the finished piece. Even the sculptures in which a section of steel has been removed often "recover" it in an inverted or displaced form (figure 4). In the nine sculptures that constitute the *Gnomon's Parade* group of 1980 (frontispiece), Wilmarth continued his emphasis on retaining the original plate. The artist wrote of the series:

> *They (these nine) have physically been the most difficult sculptures I have made as they are each pulled from a single plate of steel to support a feeling of integral and generative form. All cutting, bending, and machining was done to retain a memory of the germ—the first shape—a simple rectangle, and endow the work with a sense of expectation, as if upon returning some time later they will have continued to evolve and move.*[9]

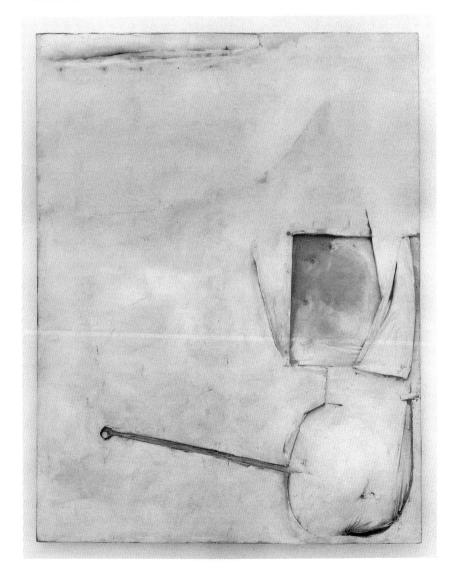

Figure 5: Hague Street Memory (For the Old Man Who Spoke with Me). *1962. Oil, nails, wire, screws, wood, and muslin stuffed with excelsior on canvas, mounted on composition board, 64³/₄ × 50¹/₈ × 2¹/₂″ (164.5 × 127.3 × 6.4 cm). Estate of Christopher Wilmarth, New York*

15

Figure 6: Filter (For Trouble). *1963. Encaustic, graphite, wire, screws, washers, nails, paper, and muslin stuffed with excelsior on board, mounted on composition board, 24¹/₈ × 17⁷/₈ × 1³/₈″ (61.3 × 45.5 × 3.5 cm). Estate of Christopher Wilmarth, New York*

The *Gnomon's Parade* family of works began in 1974 and includes *February Gnomon* (1976; plate 20), in which the steel twists diagonally on a forty-five-degree angle toward the wall. (A gnomon is the vertical plate of a sundial that casts a shadow.) While these 1980 sculptures retain the spiritual implications of "place" endowed with particular qualities of light, exemplified by the *Nine Clearings* works, in their verticality and scale they strongly suggest a human figure. Each piece "steps away" from the wall, evoking the rhythms of a marching man.

This anthropomorphic character revives tendencies found in Wilmarth's student works, such as *Hague Street Memory (For the Old Man Who Spoke with Me)* of 1962 (figure 5), which was inspired by Sunday conversations under the Brooklyn Bridge while light reflected off the water. In this creamy white canvas touched with blue, perforations and bulging relief suggest a developing human form. Another early work that exhibits a leaning toward figuration is *Filter (For Trouble)* of 1963 (figure 6). Here the ovoid—a shape Wilmarth had used as early as 1961, in the black "O" that is cut into the silvery-gray zinc plate of *The Letter "O"*—appears in triplicate.

This oval shape, in which the influence of Brancusi is again felt, recurs in a more sophisticated form in an elaborate set of works of 1979 titled *Breath* (plates 25–27). Included in the series are charcoal and pastel drawings, sculptures, etchings, paintings, and a book of poems—all inspired by the poetry of Stéphane Mallarmé, as translated by Frederick Morgan. To capture the essence of Mallarmé's poems and to affirm Mallarmé's emphasis on the spiritual, the interior, Wilmarth used a simple ovoid form, fusing the organic with the geometric and conjuring a multitude of symbols: head, soul, heart, aura, egg, germ cell, womb, cup. By suggesting both fullness and void this shape evoked the ambivalence and multiple associations of Mallarmé's words, and helped Wilmarth give form to the poet's statement that "the essence of a work consists precisely in what is not expressed."[10] Writing about Mallarmé, Wilmarth asserted: "His imagination and reverie meant more to him than anything that was actually of this world. His work is about the anguish and longing of experience not fully realized, and I found something of myself in it."[11]

To express his vision of Mallarmé's poetry, Wilmarth collaborated with master glassblower Marvin Lipofsky at the California College of Arts and Crafts and extended the metaphor of the ovoid even further. Breath, representative of the poet's life and spirit, emerges from the head and is physically blown into and received by the oval glass. As Wilmarth noted, blown glass is thus "frozen breath."[12] In *Sigh* (1979–80; plate 26), a sculpture tinged with the palest color, part of the oval's front surface is removed to resemble an open mouth, a mouth which in one deeply exhaled breath both forms the blown glass and epitomizes the run-on, extended verse of the Mallarmé poem this piece illuminates.

The works that followed the *Breath* series in the mid-eighties retained Wilmarth's figurative impulse, merging the anthropomorphic ovoid shapes, which may now be considered self-portrait heads, with the larger, more emphatically abstract "places" of his earlier sculptures, as with *Street Leaf (Mayagüez)* (1978–86; plate 29). In describing an earlier version of this subject Wilmarth wrote: "Street Leaf, / a release from confines / that light can open / when the place / remains the same / just like minds / and new thoughts / mostly moments these / sidewalk epiphanies."[13] The confinement and release Wilmarth speaks of are alluded to throughout his work, from the tightly stretched wire inset in *Hague Street Memory,* through the enveloping steel folds of *Susan Walked In* or *Gift of the Bridge,* to the spaces between the bent steel and glass of the wall reliefs. In *Doors*

Figure 7: Detail of north portal, Chartres Cathedral, in which God, creating the birds, sees Adam in his thoughts. Thirteenth century

Give Reasons (1983; plate 28) a striking white oval, mounted on a small, slanted platform of polished bronze, is placed into a cutout piece of steel that folds back on itself. *Her Sides of Me* (1983–86; plate 32), *Do Not Go Gently* (1987; plate 37), and *Self-Portrait with Sliding Light* (1987; plate 38) similarly suggest a figure caught in a constricted space. In an untitled drawing of 1987 (plate 34), one of Wilmarth's last works, two heads seem to strain against the tight rectangular shape that contains them.

This drawing, like several others executed during this time, depicts two heads placed side by side but bifurcated by an architectonic element, an image that originally appeared in Wilmarth's 1983–86 sculpture *Delancey Backs.* The image may have been inspired by a photograph the artist owned of a detail of a portal of Chartres Cathedral depicting God and Adam confined within an architectural framework (figure 7).[14] It is understandable that Wilmarth would have been attracted to this depiction of figures set in the particular place of an architectural entranceway.

In his ever more complex late pieces Wilmarth employed bronze, a material he had turned to for its coloristic qualities in the above-mentioned *Street Leaf* series of 1977, a group inspired by the crinkled autumn leaves lying on the city's sidewalks. Wilmarth exploited the patinated, earth-colored effects of bronze, which, as with the steel of *Street Leaf (Mayagüez),* he now milled, gouged, and etched with acid to record color, texture, and the artist's own touch. The material richness and tactility of these sculptures again demonstrate the painterly, textural tendencies of Wilmarth's work, evidenced earlier by the gestural nature of his etching, as well as his concern with edge and thickness, and with the juxtaposition of warm and cold colors.

In 1987, attempting in *Do Not Go Gently* to achieve the experience of light without using glass, Wilmarth made an ovoid shape out of bronze. This darkened head, anticipated in the black glass heads of *Street Leaf (Mayagüez)* and *Her Sides of Me,* is accompanied by sparklike glints of light appearing in the sheet bronze. In Wilmarth's last sculpture, *Self-Portrait with Sliding Light,* a powerful, gripping work, he encased a bronze ovoid in splattered, silvery-gray lead and set it against a striking, green-patinated bronze surface.

During the same period, shortly before his death in November 1987, Wilmarth created a series of deeply affecting, powerfully drawn images (figure 8, plates 33–36). Possibly the strongest, most beautiful works on paper he ever made, they explore a new level of expression while retaining continuity with past work. Their haunting, foreboding quality is prefigured in the grave, austere tones of some of Wilmarth's glass-and-steel structures of the seventies, while their sumptuous shading, which also recalls the luminous presence of the constructions of the seventies, brings to mind Wilmarth's student drawings. In their tactility, however, they seem more akin to the late sculptures with gouged, distressed surfaces. The dual nature of light and shadow and contrasts between abstraction and representation continue to be central concerns in these works, as the intensity and integrity of Wilmarth's vision remain always apparent.

Nevertheless, these elegiac drawings are different from the work that preceded them in important ways. Geometric and organic forms are more explicitly fused, and "place" and "person" are more clearly bound together in them than ever before. For in a remarkable progression, evident in each individual work, Wilmarth elucidated the transformation of constructivist, architectonic structure, familiar from his sculptures, into figurative shoulders and neck. Light is still assertive, although as with his late sculptures, no longer pervasive. The oval

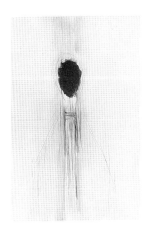

Figure 8: Untitled. 1987. Graphite, wash, and gesso on paper, 22³/₈ × 14⁷/₁₆" (56.9 × 36.8 cm). Estate of Christopher Wilmarth, New York

shapes are markedly darker, tempered only by bright shafts of light that slice through or form halos around them.

With these drawings, as throughout his oeuvre, Wilmarth created complex works that speak directly to our most profound emotions. In them the harmony and radiance of his earlier glass-and-steel sculptures, achieved through subtle arrangements of shape, proportion, color, materials, and light, give way to an intensely moving figurative expressivity. Here as before, Christopher Wilmarth's art evokes the poetry of inner longings, the mysteries of life, and the survival of the spirit.

Notes

1 Statement by Christopher Wilmarth, September 1974, printed in the catalogue *Christopher Wilmarth: Nine Clearings for a Standing Man* (Hartford: Wadsworth Atheneum, 1974), n.p.

2 See Hilton Kramer, "The Delicate Touch of a Constructivist," *The New York Times,* December 8, 1974, and Henry Geldzahler and Christopher Scott, *Christopher Wilmarth: Sculpture and Drawings* (New York: Grey Art Gallery & Study Center, New York University, 1977). I am indebted to these writers for their discussions of the relationship of Wilmarth's work to Matisse's 1914 window paintings. Geldzahler and Scott also analyze Matisse's charcoal drawings in relation to Wilmarth's art.

3 Brancusi's statement "my hands are the last hands to touch my work," cited in Dore Ashton, *Christopher Wilmarth: Layers* (New York: Hirschl & Adler Modern, 1984), p. 6, inspired the title of Wilmarth's sculpture *Last Hands.* Formed out of two sheets of glass, one shot through with a wire grid, the other textured and translucent, this work prefigures later sculptures in which Wilmarth altered the transparency of the glass and layered together different materials.

4 For an analysis of Wilmarth's use of staples, see Joseph Masheck, "Chris Wilmarth, Rosa Esman Gallery," *Artforum* (New York), vol. 12, no. 9 (May 1974), p. 66. Wilmarth's student works employ screws in a similar fashion.

5 This use of layering also figures in Wilmarth's two-dimensional art, in drawings fashioned from multiple layers of translucent paper. Wilmarth extended his layering technique by incising lines or cutting shapes out of the paper, which relates to the numerous punctures, sutures, inserts, layers, and perforations of his student pieces. The drawings in Wilmarth's 1987 series *Twelve Drawings from the Forty-fourth Year* have deep scoring that is consistent with his earlier layering methods.

6 Unpublished statement by Christopher Wilmarth, November 26, 1980. Estate of the artist, New York.

7 Statement by Christopher Wilmarth, September 1974.

8 Ibid.

9 Unpublished statement by Christopher Wilmarth, September 1980. Estate of the artist, New York.

10 Cited in Dore Ashton, "Mallarmé, Friend of Artists," *Christopher Wilmarth: Breath* (New York, 1982), p. 15.

11 Cited in Grace Glueck, "Mallarmé Poems Inspire Glass Sculpture," *The New York Times,* May 14, 1982.

12 Quoted in Alexandra Anderson, "Notes from the Art World: Meditations on Mallarmé," *Portfolio,* May/June 1982, p. 7.

13 Untitled poem by Christopher Wilmarth, printed in Susan Lubowsky, *Sculpture Since the Sixties* (New York: Whitney Museum of American Art, 1988), p. 23.

14 For information about this photograph, and for much more information shared over the course of many conversations in the spring of 1989, I am grateful to Susan Wilmarth.

PLATES

1 *Tina Turner* 1970–71

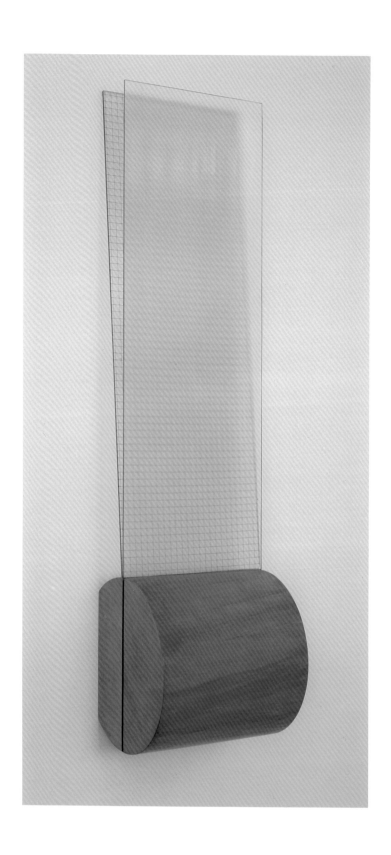

2 *Last Hands* 1969

3 *Little Bent Memphis*   1971

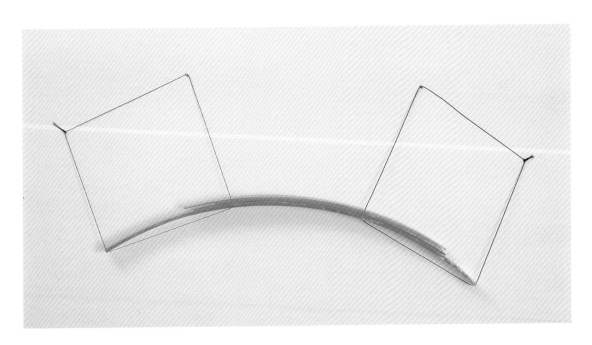

4 *Tarp*   1971

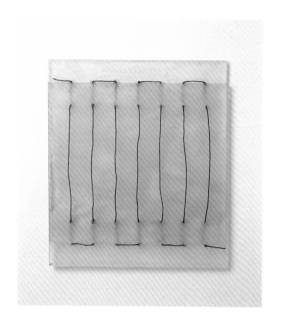

5 *Untied Drawing* 1971

6 *Lace* 1972

7 *Thinner* 1969–70

8 *Trace* 1972

9 *Susan Walked In* 1972

10 *Nine Clearings for a Standing Man #7*
1973

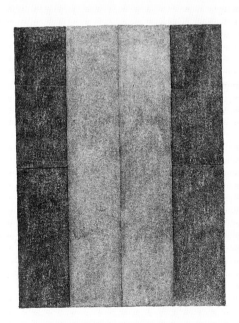

11 *Nine Clearings for a Standing Man #9*
1973

12 *Nine Clearings for a Standing Man #6* 1973

13 *Nine Clearings for a Standing Man #8*   1973

14 *Late Drawing of Wyoming*   1975

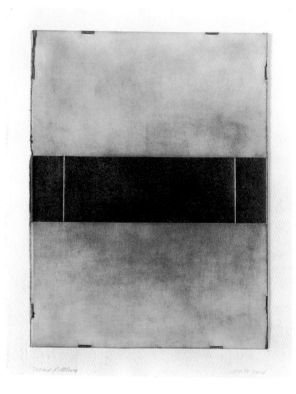

15 *Second Roebling*   1974

16 *Blue Time Line* 1974

17 Untitled c. 1976

18 *Is, Was (Chancing)* 1975−76

19 *Gift of the Bridge*   1975−76

20 *February Gnomon* 1976

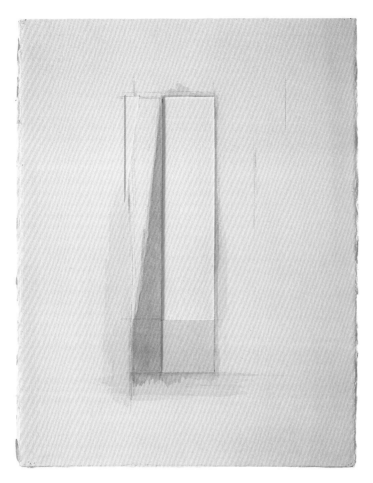

21 *Second Gnomon* 1975–76

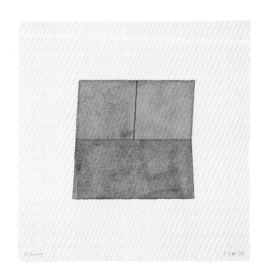

22 *Beginning* 1973

23 *Stray* 1977

24 *New Ninth* 1978

25 *"The whole soul summed up…"* 1979

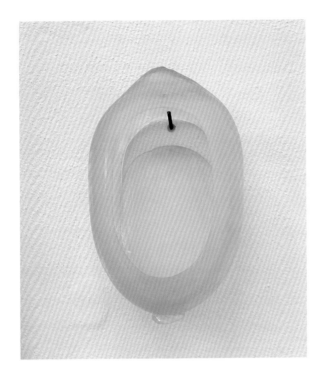

26 *Sigh* 1979–80

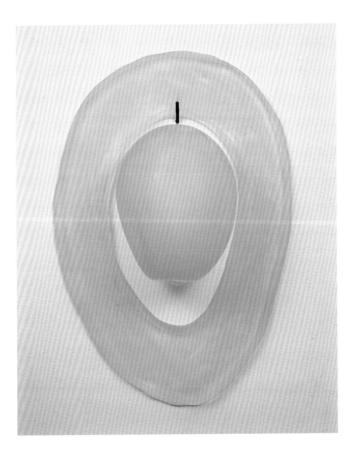

27 *"The whole soul summed up…"*
    1979–80

28 *Doors Give Reasons* 1983

29   *Street Leaf (Mayagüez)*   1978–86

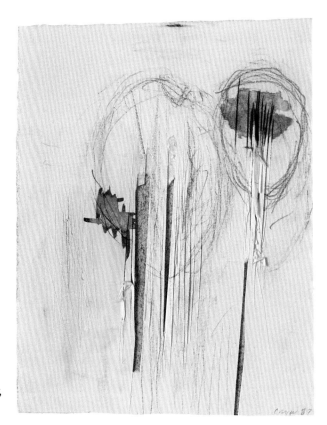

30 *Twelve Drawings from the Forty-fourth Year,*
   #2: Emanation (for Enzo & Me) 1987

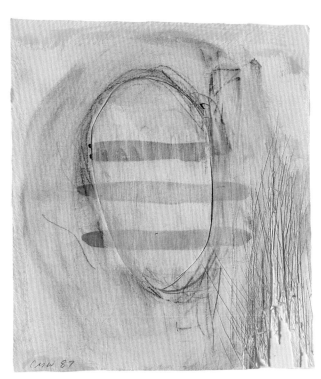

31 *Twelve Drawings from the Forty-fourth Year,*
   #9: Moment 1987

32 *Her Sides of Me* 1983 – 86

33 Untitled 1987

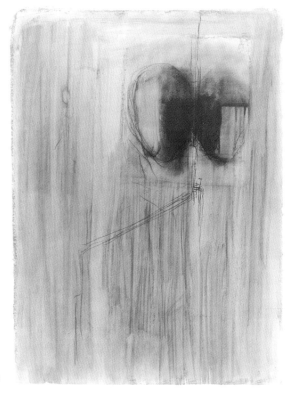

34 Untitled 1987

35 Untitled 1987

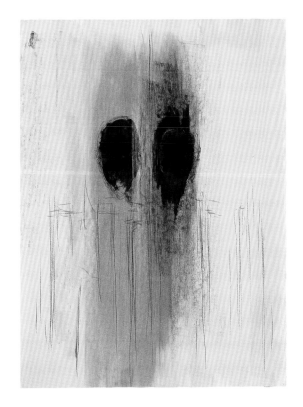

36 Untitled 1987

37 *Do Not Go Gently* 1987

38 *Self-Portrait with Sliding Light* 1987

CHECKLIST OF THE EXHIBITION

The sculptures and works on paper in the exhibition are listed below by year of completion. Dimensions are given in feet and inches, and in centimeters, height preceding width and followed by depth in the case of sculptures. Dimensions of works on paper refer to sheet size, unless otherwise specified. All works in the exhibition are reproduced in this publication, and plate references are given below.

SCULPTURES

Last Hands. 1969
Glass and wood,
48 × 12¹/₄ × 10¹/₂"
(121.9 × 31.1 × 26.7 cm)
Private collection
Plate 2

Thinner. 1969–70
Glass and steel rods,
14" × 46⁵/₈" × 6'
(35.5 × 118.5 × 182.8 cm)
Estate of Christopher Wilmarth,
    New York
Plate 7

Tina Turner. 1970–71
Etched glass, glass, and steel cable,
69³/₄" × 14'9" × 58"
(177.2 × 449.6 × 147.4 cm)
The Edward R. Broida Trust,
    Los Angeles
Plate 1

Little Bent Memphis. 1971
Etched glass and steel cable,
42" × 7'8" × 5"
(106.8 × 233.7 × 12.7 cm)
The Edward R. Broida Trust,
    Los Angeles
Plate 3

Tarp. 1971
Etched glass and steel cable,
26¹/₄ × 68¹/₂ × 4¹/₂"
(66.5 × 174 × 11.4 cm)
The Museum of Modern Art, New
    York. Advisory Committee Fund
Plate 4

Untied Drawing. 1971
Etched glass and steel cable,
19 × 17 × 1" (48.2 × 43.2 × 2.5 cm)
Collection George G. Hadley and
    Richard L. Solomon
Plate 5

Lace. 1972
Etched glass and steel cable,
16 × 16 × 2⁷/₈"
(40.7 × 40.7 × 7.3 cm)
Estate of Christopher Wilmarth,
    New York
Plate 6

Trace. 1972
Etched glass, steel, and steel cable,
60 × 60 × 36"
(152.4 × 152.4 × 91.4 cm)
Walker Art Center, Minneapolis
    Purchased with the aid of funds
    from the National Endowment for
    the Arts and gifts from Mr. and
    Mrs. Edmond R. Ruben, Mr. and
    Mrs. Julius E. Davis, Suzanne
    Walker, and Thomas Gilmore
Plate 8

Susan Walked In. 1972
Etched glass, steel, and steel cable,
60 × 60 × 30"
(152.3 × 152.3 × 76.2 cm)
Collection Susan Wilmarth,
    New York
Plate 9

*Nine Clearings for a
    Standing Man #6.* 1973
Etched glass, steel, and steel cable,
6'8" × 60" × 4³/₄"
(203.2 × 152.4 × 12 cm)
Philadelphia Museum of Art
    Purchased with a grant from the
    National Endowment for the
    Arts and funds contributed by
    private donors
Plate 12

*Nine Clearings for a
    Standing Man #8.* 1973
Etched glass, steel, and steel cable,
6'8" × 60" × 3¹/₂"
(203.2 × 152.4 × 8.9 cm)
Estate of Christopher Wilmarth,
    New York
Plate 13

Blue Time Line. 1974
Etched glass and steel cable,
6'6" × 38" × 7¹/₄"
(198.1 × 96.4 × 18.5 cm)
Estate of Chrisopher Wilmarth,
    New York
Plate 16

Is, Was (Chancing). 1975–76
Etched glass, steel, and steel cable,
40 × 63¹/₂ × 30"
(101.6 × 161.3 × 76.2 cm)
Estate of Christopher Wilmarth,
    New York
Plate 18

Gift of the Bridge. 1975–76
Etched glass and steel,
6' × 6' × 48"
(182.8 × 182.8 × 121.9 cm)
Wadsworth Atheneum, Hartford
    The National Endowment for the
    Arts Museum Purchase Plan with
    matching funds bequeathed by
    Roscoe Nelson Gray in memory of
    Roscoe Nelson Dalton Gray and
    Rene Gabrielle Gray
Plate 19

February Gnomon. 1976
Etched glass and steel,
8' × 30" × 11"
(243.9 × 76.2 × 28 cm)
The Edward R. Broida Trust,
    Los Angeles
Plate 20

Stray. 1977
Etched glass, steel, and steel cable,
42 × 42 × 3"
(106.8 × 106.8 × 7.8 cm)
Collection Stephen D. Weinroth,
    New York
Plate 23

New Ninth. 1978
Etched glass, steel, and steel cable,
40 × 32 × 6"
(101.6 × 81.3 × 15.2 cm)
Private collection, New York
Plate 24

Sigh. 1979–80
Etched glass,
13 × 7³/₄ × 6"
(33 × 19.7 × 15.2 cm)
Estate of Christopher Wilmarth,
    New York
Plate 26

"The whole soul summed up…"
1979–80
Etched glass,
17 × 12 × 5¹/₄"
(43.2 × 30.5 × 13.3 cm)
Collection Robert and
    Marlene Baumgarten
Plate 27

Gnomon's Parade (Front). 1980
Etched glass and steel,
8'3" × 36" × 52"
(251.5 × 91.4 × 132.1 cm)
Courtesy Hirschl & Adler Modern,
    New York
Frontispiece

Doors Give Reasons. 1983
Etched glass, steel, and bronze,
30 × 20 × 6³/₄"
(76.2 × 50.8 × 17.2 cm)
Collection Mr. and
    Mrs. David Pincus
Plate 28

Street Leaf (Mayagüez). 1978–86
Etched glass, steel, and steel cable,
48" × 6' × 9"
(122 × 182.8 × 22.8 cm)
Collection Asher B. Edelman,
    New York
Plate 29

Her Sides of Me. 1983–86
Etched glass, steel, and bronze,
6' × 41¹/₂" × 8"
(182.8 × 105.2 × 20.3 cm)
The Edward R. Broida Trust,
    Los Angeles
Plate 32

Do Not Go Gently. 1987
Bronze and steel,
48 × 18 × 4"
(121.9 × 45.8 × 10.2 cm)
Collection Robert Lehrman,
    Washington, D.C.
Plate 37

Self-Portrait with Sliding Light. 1987
Steel, bronze, and lead,
53¹/₄ × 17 × 7¹/₄"
(135.2 × 43.2 × 18.4 cm)
Estate of Christopher Wilmarth,
    New York
Plate 38

WORKS ON PAPER

*Nine Clearings for a
    Standing Man #7*. 1973
Watercolor and graphite on paper,
13¹¹/₁₆ × 11¹/₄" (34.9 × 28.7 cm)
Estate of Christopher Wilmarth,
    New York
Plate 10

*Nine Clearings for a
    Standing Man #9*. 1973
Watercolor and graphite on paper,
13¹/₂ × 11¹/₄" (34.4 × 28.7 cm)
Estate of Christopher Wilmarth,
    New York
Plate 11

Beginning. 1973
Watercolor and graphite on paper,
10¹/₈ × 10" (25.7 × 25.4 cm)
Estate of Christopher Wilmarth,
    New York
Plate 22

Second Roebling. 1974
Graphite on layered paper and vellum
    with staples, mounted on paper;
12 × 9¹/₈" (30.5 × 23.3 cm),
    mount 14³/₈ × 11¹/₄"
    (36.1 × 28.7 cm)
Estate of Christopher Wilmarth,
    New York
Plate 15

Late Drawing of Wyoming. 1975
Graphite on layered paper with
    staples,
18¹/₈ × 22³/₄" (46.1 × 57.9 cm)
Estate of Christopher Wilmarth,
    New York
Plate 14

Second Gnomon. 1975–76
Watercolor and graphite on
    layered paper,
29¹/₈ × 22³/₄" (74 × 57.9 cm)
Estate of Christopher Wilmarth,
    New York
Plate 21

Untitled. c. 1976
Graphite and wash on vellum,
29 × 22" (73.8 × 56 cm)
Estate of Christopher Wilmarth,
    New York
Plate 17

"The whole soul summed up…". 1979
Pastel and graphite on layered paper,
26³/₈ × 19¹/₄" (66.6 × 49 cm)
Estate of Christopher Wilmarth,
    New York
Plate 25

*Twelve Drawings from the Forty-fourth
    Year, #2: Emanation (for Enzo &
    Me)*. 1987
Graphite, ink, and gesso on layered
    paper, mounted on paper;
8 × 6¹/₄" (20.4 × 16 cm),
    mount 13 × 11" (33 × 28 cm)
Courtesy Hirschl & Adler Modern,
    New York
Plate 30

*Twelve Drawings from the Forty-fourth
    Year, #9: Moment*. 1987
Graphite, ink, gesso, and rabbitskin
    glue on layered paper, mounted
    on paper;
7¹/₁₆ × 6¹/₄" (18 × 16 cm),
    mount 13 × 11" (33 × 28 cm)
Courtesy Hirschl & Adler Modern,
    New York
Plate 31

Untitled. 1987
Graphite, wash, gesso, and rabbit-
    skin glue on paper,
30 × 42" (76.3 × 106.8 cm)
Estate of Christopher Wilmarth,
    New York
Plate 33

Untitled. 1987
Graphite, wash, and gesso on paper,
31 × 22⁵/₈" (78.8 × 57.5 cm)
Estate of Christopher Wilmarth,
    New York
Plate 34

Untitled. 1987
Graphite, wash, and rabbitskin glue
    on paper,
30⁷/₈ × 22¹/₈" (78.5 × 56.2 cm)
Estate of Christopher Wilmarth,
    New York
Plate 35

Untitled. 1987
Graphite, wash, and rabbitskin glue
    on paper,
30 × 22³/₈" (76.2 × 56.9 cm)
Estate of Christopher Wilmarth,
    New York
Plate 36

Christopher Wilmarth, Sackett Street studio, Brooklyn, 1986.
Photo: Jerry L. Thompson, Amenia, New York

CHRONOLOGY

1943

Born June 11, Sonoma, California.

1960

To New York City.

1965

B.F.A., The Cooper Union for the Advancement of Science and Art, New York.

1967

Studio assistant to Tony Smith, to 1969.

1969

National Endowment for the Arts Grant.

Professor of Sculpture and Drawing, The Cooper Union for the Advancement of Science and Art, New York, to 1980.

1970–71

John Simon Guggenheim Memorial Foundation Fellowship.

1971–72

Visiting Artist, Yale University, New Haven.

1972

Norman Wait Harris Award, The Art Institute of Chicago.

Howard Foundation Fellowship, Brown University, Providence.

1973

Worked in Milan, January–April.

1974

Traveled to Tirgu-Jiu, Rumania, summer, to visit site of Brancusi's public sculptures.

1976

Visiting Artist, Columbia University, New York, to 1978.

1977

National Endowment for the Arts Grant.

1978

Founded The Studio for the First Amendment, 144 Wooster Street, New York, January 7.

1979

Visiting Artist, University of California at Berkeley.

Learned glassblowing from Marvin Lipofsky at California College of Arts and Crafts, Oakland.

1980

National Endowment for the Arts Grant.

New York State Council on the Arts C.A.P.S. Grant.

1982

Visited Chartres Cathedral, summer.

1983

Closed The Studio for the First Amendment, January 7.

1983–84

John Simon Guggenheim Memorial Foundation Fellowship.

1984

Moved studio to Sackett Street in the Red Hook section of Brooklyn, September.

1986

Professor of Sculpture, Columbia University, New York.

1987

Died November 19.

EXHIBITIONS

Exhibition dates are listed when known. A star in the entry indicates a catalogue or brochure accompanied the exhibition.

ONE-MAN EXHIBITIONS

1968

Graham Gallery, New York. "Christopher Wilmarth,"★ October 26 – November 23. See bibl. 13, 41.

1971

Paula Cooper Gallery, New York. "Chris Wilmarth: Sculpture," March 14 – April 7. See bibl. 33.

Janie C. Lee Gallery, Dallas. "Chris Wilmarth," opened November 20.

1972

Paula Cooper Gallery, New York. "Chris Wilmarth," March 11 – April 5. See bibl. 27.

1973

Galleria dell'Ariete, Milan. "Chris Wilmarth Sculpture,"★ opened April 3.

1974

Rosa Esman Gallery, New York. "Chris Wilmarth: Drawings and Small Sculptures," February 2 – 28. See bibl. 28.

Daniel Weinberg Gallery, San Francisco. "Chris Wilmarth: Recent Sculpture," March 5 – 30. See bibl. 7, 30.

Wadsworth Atheneum, Hartford. "Christopher Wilmarth: Nine Clearings for a Standing Man,"★ November 13, 1974 – January 12, 1975. Traveled to The St. Louis Art Museum, February 6 – March 20, 1975. See bibl. 21, 23, 29, 46.

1975

Galerie Aronowitsch, Stockholm. "Chris Wilmarth," April – May.

1977

Wadsworth Atheneum, Hartford. "Christopher Wilmarth: Matrix 29,"★ February – mid-April. See bibl. 26, 47.

1978

The Studio for the First Amendment, New York. "Christopher Wilmarth: Recent Sculpture," January 10 – February 4. See bibl. 10, 20, 22, 36.

Grey Art Gallery & Study Center, New York University, New York. "Christopher Wilmarth: Sculpture and Drawings,"★ January 10 – February 10. See bibl. 10, 12, 20, 22, 36.

Daniel Weinberg Gallery, San Francisco. "Chris Wilmarth: Recent Sculpture and Drawings," opened September 11. See bibl. 31.

André Emmerich Gallery, New York. "Christopher Wilmarth: Sculpture 1972 – 1973," September 12 – October 4. See bibl. 48.

1979

Seattle Art Museum. "Christopher Wilmarth,"★ January 25 – March 25.

1980

The Studio for the First Amendment, New York. "Christopher Wilmarth: Gnomon's Parade," November 8 – December 6. See bibl. 3.

1982

The Studio for the First Amendment, New York. "Christopher Wilmarth: Breath,"★ May 1 – 29. Traveled to Institute of Contemporary Art, Boston, closed May 1, 1983; University Art Museum, Berkeley, late May – August 7, 1983; University Art Museum, Santa Barbara, January 4 – February 5, 1984. See bibl. 4, 15, 25, 40.

1984

Hirschl & Adler Modern, New York. "Christopher Wilmarth: Layers, Works from 1961 – 1984,"★ March 17 – April 19. See bibl. 2, 8, 14, 18.

1986

Hirschl & Adler Modern, New York. "Chris Wilmarth: Delancey Backs (and Other Moments),"★ November 1 – December 3. See bibl. 19, 32, 38, 39.

1989

Neuberger Museum, State University of New York at Purchase. "Christopher Wilmarth/Days on Blue 1977," January 21, 1989 – January 7, 1990.

GROUP EXHIBITIONS

1966

Park Place Gallery, New York. Invitational exhibition, June 12 – 30.

Whitney Museum of American Art, New York. "Annual Exhibition 1966: Contemporary Sculpture and Prints,"★ December 16, 1966 – February 5, 1967.

1967

Graham Gallery, New York.

1968

The Aldrich Museum of Contemporary Art, Ridgefield, Connecticut. "Cool Art—1967,"★ January 7 – March 17.

The Newark Museum, Newark, New Jersey. "Cool Art: Abstraction Today,"★ May 27 – September 29.

Whitney Museum of American Art, New York. "1968 Annual Exhibition: Contemporary American Sculpture,"★ December 17, 1968 – February 9, 1969.

1969

Graham Gallery, New York. "The Big Drawing," April 8 – May 3.

The Jewish Museum, New York. "Superlimited: Books, Boxes and Things,"★ April 16 – June 29.

The Aldrich Museum of Contemporary Art, Ridgefield, Connecticut. "Highlights of the 1968 – 1969 Art Season," June 22 – September 14.

Paula Cooper Gallery, New York.

1970

French & Co., New York. "Tom Clancy and Chris Wilmarth," June 20 – August 31.

Fondation Maeght, Saint-Paul-de-Vence, France. "L'Art vivant aux Etats-Unis,"★ July 16 – September 30.

Paula Cooper Gallery, New York. "Art for Peace," exhibition sponsored by Referendum 70, September 19 – 26.

The New Gallery, Cleveland. "Small Works," opened December 4.

Whitney Museum of American Art, New York. "1970 Annual Exhibition: Contemporary American Sculpture,"★ December 12, 1970 – February 7, 1971.

Janie C. Lee Gallery, Dallas.

1971

Vassar College Art Gallery, Poughkeepsie, New York. "Twenty-six by Twenty-six,"★ May 1 – June 6.

The Aldrich Museum of Contemporary Art, Ridgefield, Connecticut. "Highlights of the 1970 – 1971 Art Season," June 27 – September 19.

The Museum of Modern Art, New York. "Recent Acquisitions IX," October 7 – 14, October 27, 1971 – January 2, 1972.

Utah Museum of Fine Arts, University of Utah, Salt Lake City. "Drawings by New York Artists,"★ November 28, 1971 – January 12, 1972. Traveled to Henry Gallery, University of Washington, Seattle; Arizona State University, Tempe; Georgia Museum of Art, University of Georgia, Athens; Finch College Museum of Art, New York; Hayden Gallery, Massachusetts Institute of Technology, Cambridge.

Windham College, Putney, Vermont.

1972

Storm King Art Center, Mountainville, New York. "Painting and Sculpture, 1972," April 8 – June 11.

The Indianapolis Museum of Art. "Painting and Sculpture Today 1972,"★ April 26 – June 4.

The Art Institute of Chicago. "Seventieth American Exhibition,"★ June 24 – August 20.

1973

Whitney Museum of American Art, New York. "1973 Biennial Exhibition: Contemporary American Art,"★ January 10 – March 18.

Museum of Art, Rhode Island School of Design, Providence. "The Albert Pilavin Collection: Twentieth-Century American Art II,"★ October 23 – November 25.

Paula Cooper Gallery, New York. "Drawings and Other Works," December 15, 1973 – January 9, 1974.

Studio Marconi, Milan.

1974

The Metropolitan Museum of Art, New York. "20th-Century Art Accessions 1967 – 1974," March 14 – April 24.

The Sarah Lawrence College Art Gallery, Bronxville, New York. "Questions Answers," April 16 – 26.

The Indianapolis Museum of Art. "Painting and Sculpture Today 1974,"★ May 22 – July 14.

Sculpture Now, New York. Inaugural exhibition, November 1974 – January 1975.

1975

Hayward Gallery, London. "The Condition of Sculpture,"★ exhibition organized by the Arts Council of Great Britain, May 29 – July 13.

1976

Whitney Museum of American Art, New York. "200 Years of American Sculpture,"★ March 16 – September 26.

Grey Art Gallery & Study Center, New York University, New York. "Project Rebuild," August 11 – 27.

1977

Museum of Contemporary Art, Chicago. "'A View of a Decade,'"★ September 10 – November 10.

John Weber Gallery, New York. "Drawings for Outdoor Sculpture 1946–1977,"★ October 29– November 23. Traveled to Mead Art Museum, Amherst College, Amherst, Massachusetts; University Art Museum, Santa Barbara; La Jolla Museum of Contemporary Art, La Jolla, California; Hayden Gallery, Massachusetts Institute of Technology, Cambridge.

Los Angeles County Museum of Art. "Private Images: Photographs by Sculptors,"★ December 20, 1977– March 5, 1978.

1978

Philadelphia Museum of Art. "8 Artists,"★ April 29–June 25. See bibl. 17.

Huntington Museum of Art, Huntington, West Virginia. "Dialogue," September 29– November 26.

1979

Rosa Esman Gallery, New York. "Places to Be: Unrealized Monumental Projects," January 9– February 3.

Whitney Museum of American Art, New York. "1979 Biennial Exhibition,"★ February 6–April 8.

Albright-Knox Art Gallery, Buffalo. "Eight Sculptors,"★ March 17– April 29. See bibl. 37.

The Museum of Modern Art, New York. "Contemporary Sculpture: Selections from the Collection of The Museum of Modern Art,"★ May 18– August 7.

Whitney Museum of American Art, New York. "The Decade in Review: Selections from the 1970s,"★ June 19– September 2.

The Metropolitan Museum of Art, New York. "Recent Acquisitions," October 16, 1979–January 1980.

1980

Grey Art Gallery & Study Center, New York University, New York. "Perceiving Modern Sculpture: Selections for the Sighted and Non-Sighted," July 8–August 22.

Comune di Udine, Civici Musei e Gallerie di Storia e Arte, Udine, Italy. "Arte americana contemporanea,"★ September 20–November 16.

1981

The Cleveland Museum of Art. "Contemporary Artists,"★ October 21–November 29.

1982

City Gallery, New York City Department of Cultural Affairs, New York. "Made in New York," February 1–17. Traveled to The Bronx Museum of the Arts, March 25–April 29.

Yale University Art Gallery, New Haven. "Prints by Contemporary Sculptors,"★ May 18–August 31.

Museum of Art, Carnegie Institute, Pittsburgh. "1982 Carnegie International,"★ October 23, 1982– January 2, 1983. Traveled to Seattle Art Museum, February 10– March 27, 1983. Australian tour, June–November 1983: Art Gallery of Western Australia, Perth; National Gallery of Victoria, Melbourne; Art Gallery of New South Wales, Sydney.

Emily Lowe Gallery, Hofstra University, Hempstead, New York. "Androgyny in Art,"★ November 6– December 19.

1983

Whitney Museum of American Art, New York. "Minimalism to Expressionism,"★ June 2– December 4.

"American Accents,"★ exhibition sponsored by Rothmans of Pall Mall Canada Limited. Traveled to nine museums in Canada, June 6, 1983– January 30, 1985. See bibl. 11.

Grey Art Gallery & Study Center, New York University, New York. "The Permanent Collection: Highlights and Recent Acquisitions," November 8–December 10.

1984

The Museum of Modern Art, New York. "An International Survey of Recent Painting and Sculpture,"★ May 17–August 19.

1985

The Hudson River Museum, Yonkers, New York. "A New Beginning: 1968–1978,"★ February 3– May 5. See bibl. 9.

Hill Gallery, Birmingham, Michigan. "Image and Mystery," April 21– May 30.

The Brooklyn Museum, New York. "Working in Brooklyn/Sculpture,"★ October 18, 1985–January 6, 1986.

1986

Hirschl & Adler Modern, New York. "Cy Twombly, Christopher Wilmarth, Joe Zucker,"★ May 21– June 27.

Arnold Herstand and Company, New York. "American Sculpture: A Selection," June 4–July 31.

John Berggruen Gallery, San Francisco. "Sculpture and Works in Relief,"★ October 9–November 29.

Marian Locks Gallery, Philadelphia. "The Purist Image,"★ November 1–30.

1987

The Corcoran Gallery of Art, Washington, D.C. "Spectrum: Three Sculptors,"★ May 9–August 16. See bibl. 6.

Michael Walls Gallery, New York. "Beyond Reductive Tendencies," September 12–October 3.

1988

Whitney Museum of American Art at Equitable Center, New York. "Sculpture Since the Sixties,"★ August 18, 1988–August 9, 1989. See bibl. 24.

1989

Hirschl & Adler Modern, New York. "Repetition,"★ February 25– March 25.

SELECTED BIBLIOGRAPHY

1. Anderson, Alexandra. "Christopher Wilmarth: Portfolio," *The Paris Review* (New York), vol. 15, no. 58 (Summer 1974), pp. 102–10.

2. Ashton, Dore. "Christopher Wilmarth: Layers." *Christopher Wilmarth: Layers, Works from 1961–1984* [catalogue]. New York: Hirschl & Adler Modern, 1984.

3. _____. "Christopher Wilmarth's Gnomic Sculpture," *Arts Magazine* (New York), vol. 55, no. 4 (December 1980), cover, pp. 93–95.

4. _____. "Mallarmé, Friend of Artists." *Christopher Wilmarth: Breath.* Inspired by seven poems of Stéphane Mallarmé translated by Frederick Morgan [catalogue]. Published 1982 in connection with the exhibition "Christopher Wilmarth: Breath" at The Studio for the First Amendment, New York.

5. _____. "Radiance and Reserve: The Sculpture of Christopher Wilmarth," *Arts Magazine* (New York), vol. 45, no. 5 (March 1971), pp. 31–33.

6. Beardsley, John. *Three Sculptors* [catalogue]. Washington, D.C.: The Corcoran Gallery of Art, 1987.

7. Butterfield, Jan. "New Beauty" [exhibition review, Daniel Weinberg Gallery], *Pacific Sun* (Mill Valley, Calif.), March 28–April 3, 1974.

8. Cohen, Ronny. "Christopher Wilmarth: Hirschl & Adler Modern" [exhibition review], *Art News* (New York), vol. 83, no. 6 (Summer 1984), pp. 185–86.

9. Delahoyd, Mary. *A New Beginning: 1968–1978* [catalogue]. Yonkers, N.Y.: The Hudson River Museum, 1985.

10. Dietz, Paula. "Constructing Inner Space," *New York Arts Journal* (New York), no. 9 (April/May 1978), pp. 26–28.

11. Geldzahler, Henry. *American Accents* [catalogue]. Canada: Rothmans of Pall Mall Canada Limited, 1983.

12. Geldzahler, Henry, and Christopher Scott. *Christopher Wilmarth: Sculpture and Drawings* [brochure]. New York: Grey Art Gallery & Study Center, New York University, 1977.

13. Glueck, Grace. "Christopher Wilmarth: Graham Gallery" [exhibition review], *Art in America* (New York), vol. 56, no. 5 (September/October 1968), p. 112.

14. _____. "Christopher Wilmarth's 'Layers'" [exhibition review, Hirschl & Adler Modern], *The New York Times,* March 23, 1984.

15. _____. "Mallarmé Poems Inspire Glass Sculpture" [exhibition review, The Studio for the First Amendment], *The New York Times,* May 14, 1982.

16. Hagenberg, Roland. "Chris Wilmarth: The Sun Is Just a Square Upon the Wall," *New Art International* (Paris), no. 1 (February/March 1988), pp. 43–46. Previously printed in *Art Finder* (New York), Spring 1987, pp. 60–65. See also bibl. 43.

17. d'Harnoncourt, Anne. *8 Artists* [brochure]. Philadelphia: Philadelphia Museum of Art, 1978.

18. Henry, Gerrit. "Christopher Wilmarth at Hirschl & Adler Modern" [exhibition review], *Art in America* (New York), vol. 72, no. 8 (September 1984), pp. 212–13.

19. Hirschl & Adler Modern. *Chris Wilmarth: Delancey Backs (and Other Moments)* [catalogue]. New York: Hirschl & Adler Modern, 1986.

20. Kramer, Hilton. "Christopher Wilmarth" [exhibition review, Grey Art Gallery & Study Center and The Studio for the First Amendment], *The New York Times,* January 20, 1978.

21. _____. "The Delicate Touch of a Constructivist" [exhibition review, Wadsworth Atheneum], *The New York Times,* December 8, 1974.

22. Larson, Philip. "Christopher Wilmarth at N.Y.U.'s Grey Gallery and the 'Studio for the First Amendment'" [exhibition review], *Art in America* (New York), vol. 66, no. 3 (May/June 1978), p. 117.

23. Linker, Kate. "Christopher Wilmarth: Nine Clearings for a Standing Man," *Arts Magazine* (New York), vol. 49, no. 8 (April 1975), cover, pp. 52–53.

24. Lubowsky, Susan. *Sculpture Since the Sixties* [catalogue]. New York: Whitney Museum of American Art, 1988.

25. Madoff, Steven Henry. "Christopher Wilmarth at the Studio for the First Amendment" [exhibition review], *Art in America* (New York), vol. 70, no. 10 (November 1982), pp. 119–20.

26. Marlow, Peter O. *Christopher Wilmarth: Matrix 29* [brochure]. Hartford: Wadsworth Atheneum, 1977. Includes bibl. 47.

27. Masheck, Joseph. "Chris Wilmarth" [exhibition review, Paula Cooper Gallery], *Artforum* (New York), vol. 10, no. 10 (June 1972), p. 81.

28. _____. "Chris Wilmarth, Rosa Esman Gallery" [exhibition review], *Artforum* (New York), vol. 12, no. 9 (May 1974), pp. 65–66.

29. _____. "Wilmarth's New Reliefs." *Christopher Wilmarth: Nine Clearings for a Standing Man* [catalogue]. Hartford: Wadsworth Atheneum, 1974. See also bibl. 46.

30. McDonald, Robert. "Chris Wilmarth" [exhibition review, Daniel Weinberg Gallery], *Artweek* (Oakland, Calif.), vol. 5, no. 12 (March 23, 1974), p. 5.

31. _____. "Rich Effects in Steel and Glass" [exhibition review, Daniel Weinberg Gallery], *Artweek* (Oakland, Calif.), vol. 9, no. 32 (September 30, 1978), p. 1.

32. Megged, Matti. "The Void and the Dream: New Sculptures by Christopher Wilmarth," *Arts Magazine* (New York), vol. 61, no. 10 (June/Summer 1987), pp. 74–75.

33. Pincus-Witten, Robert. "Christopher Wilmarth, A Note on Pictorial Sculpture," *Artforum* (New York), vol. 9, no. 9 (May 1971), pp. 54–56.

34. Poirier, Maurice. "Christopher Wilmarth: 'The Medium Is Light,'" *Art News* (New York), vol. 84, no. 10 (December 1985), pp. 68–75.

35. Robins, Corinne. "The Circle in Orbit," *Art in America* (New York), vol. 56, no. 6 (November/December 1968), pp. 62–63. Includes bibl. 45.

36. Rubinfien, Leo. "Christopher Wilmarth, Grey Art Gallery, N.Y.U., and Studio for the First Amendment" [exhibition review], *Artforum* (New York), vol. 16, no. 7 (March 1978), pp. 70–72.

37. Schultz, Douglas G. *Eight Sculptors* [catalogue]. Buffalo: Albright-Knox Art Gallery, 1979.

38. Schwabsky, Barry. "Chris Wilmarth" [exhibition review, Hirschl & Adler Modern], *Arts Magazine* (New York), vol. 61, no. 5 (January 1987), p. 121.

39. Smith, Roberta. "Chris Wilmarth" [exhibition review, Hirschl & Adler Modern], *The New York Times,* November 7, 1986.

40. Taylor, Robert. "Christopher Wilmarth: Breath" [exhibition review, Institute of Contemporary Art, Boston], *The Boston Globe,* April 10, 1983.

41. Wasserman, Emily. "Christopher Wilmarth, Graham Gallery" [exhibition review], *Artforum* (New York), vol. 7, no. 5 (January 1969), pp. 59–60.

42. Wilmarth, Christopher. *Breath.* Inspired by seven poems of Stéphane Mallarmé translated by Frederick Morgan. A limited edition containing seven poems by Christopher Wilmarth, published New York, 1982. Reprinted in *Poetry East* (Charlottesville, Va.), nos. 13 & 14 (Spring/Summer 1984), pp. 174–76.

43. _____. "Chris Wilmarth: The Sun Is Just a Square Upon the Wall" [interview with Roland Hagenberg]. Printed 1988 in bibl. 16.

44. _____. "Pages, Places, and Dreams (or The Search for Jackson Island)," *Poetry East* (Charlottesville, Va.), nos. 13 & 14 (Spring/Summer 1984), pp. 171–73.

45. _____. [Statement]. Printed 1968 in bibl. 35.

46. _____. [Statement]. September 1974. Printed 1974 in catalogue cited in bibl. 29.

47. _____. "The True Story of the Gift of the Bridge." Written in Milan, 1973, rewritten in New York, 1977. Printed 1977 in bibl. 26.

48. Zucker, Barbara. "Christopher Wilmarth" [exhibition review, André Emmerich Gallery], *Art News* (New York), vol. 77, no. 9 (November 1978), p. 181.

TRUSTEES OF
THE MUSEUM OF MODERN ART